NOTICE ME

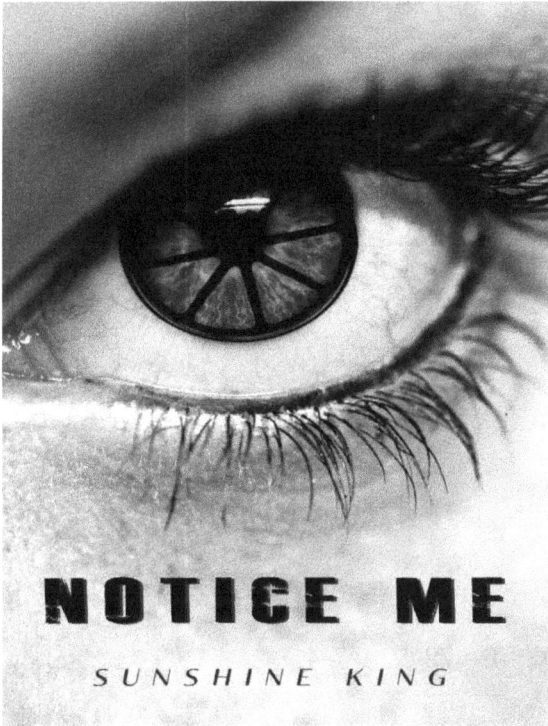

WRITTEN BY

Sunshine King

Notice Me

Notice Me © 2017

by Sunshine King

ISBN 978-0-578-52827-4

Dedication

For my son Isaiah D. Martin

I would like to dedicate this book to my wonderful son Isaiah D. Martin who stayed strong through the catastrophic times in our life. You mean the world to me and as your mother I want the very best for you. I'm just glad that you stayed mentally and spiritually strong. Just remember, don't allow anything to break you, because you are an amazing young man with a big heart. Wake up everyday thankful and grateful because as I always say, "New Day New Beginnings" and "Life can be hard at times Just don't make it harder than it has to be."

~~~Love always, Mom

Notice Me

TABLE OF CONTENTS

Notice Me

Prelude

The sun was barely out; the air dry and crisp. I left my home happy and prepared to go to work. Then, he was there. A man, all in black. He was holding a gun. Startled, I couldn't believe what I was seeing. He began screaming wildly, waving a gun at me. I was petrified. With every word he uttered, I could see the fury boil within him.

As I stood there, in shock, he just kept yelling. Then he rammed the cold barrel of the gun into my face, demanding I go with him. Summoning every bit of courage, I flatly refused. Instead, I tried to flee, throwing what I had in hand at him as a distraction.

The distraction didn't' work.

Suddenly, my body stiffened as I fell to the ground. I was terrified to move. Then he was there, hovering over me; the gun still glued in his hand. He continued screaming, madness making his words incoherent. He was frantic and out of control.

As quickly as he started, he stopped. There was silence. He then moved closer, and fear overtook me. I had no idea what he intended to do next. To my horror and complete surprise, he leaned down placing the gun to my head and did the unthinkable. All I could do at that moment was to lay there and pray to God.

Then he turned away, distracted by someone. He turned the gun on them, his maddened words threating a new target. I prayed that he would not succumb to that madness, and hurt the person that had taken his attention away from me. Yet, I took this as my chance to run or become a distraction for the other person. No matter what, we were at the mercy of his gun.

Sunshine King

My movement caught his attention. He turned
quickly toward me; I was once again his target.

Bang!
Bang!
Bang!
Bang!

Again, I fell to the ground. Coldness pooled
around me. And then, he was gone.

Notice Me

Chapter 1

In Seconds

Although what you just read seems fantastical, a story of fiction, I assure you, it is not. I was assaulted by a man with a gun. In seconds, my life was forever changed.

I awoke. My vision was distorted; unclear. My body shifted, but not of my own control. Someone was pushing me. Suddenly, noise erupted all around me; and I was lost in an explosion of chaos and confusion. Two individuals came into view, hovering over me, pushing and pulling at my body. One, a male from the sound of his deep voice, removed my wedding band stating that I no longer needed it.

All I could do was think. *What is going on? Where am I? What happened to me?* Then everything went black.

When I woke for the second time, I was in a room filled with people. There was family, friends, and coworkers. I saw them all. Soon a doctor came in explaining that I would have to go up for surgery. A surgery to have braces installed to fix my damaged jaw. Even though, I was present for all this, though my body was there, my mind was consumed in a blur of perplexity.

In the back of my mind, I *knew* what had happened to me, but I couldn't understand *why* it happened. Again, my mind wondered. Though the question of why eluded me. I knew in those few seconds that my life would never be the same. Again, darkness took hold.

The third time I awoke, I felt like I was spinning around in circles. Lying in a hospital bed, I notice that my legs were enclosed by compression boots. Family and friends stood over me with blank yet hopeful stares, with praying eyes, and mournful hearts. It felt like I could not to get a moment to myself. So many people were coming in and out of the room— doctors, nurses, family, and friends. My world was in a whirlwind.

Yet, again, all I could do was think. *Why? Why did this happen to me?*

Later that evening, after visiting hours a pain overtook me. It was an intense pain deep in my chest. When I voiced this to the nurse, he said not to worry about it; that there was a chest tube in my chest. *What, a chest tube?*

Common knowledge is that a chest tube is a flexible plastic tube that is inserted through the chest cavity into the space between your lungs in effort to remove foreign objects such as excess air, fluid, or pus. In my case, it was fluid. This knowledge was alien to me at the time. The question of why I had a chest tube in the first place was fore front in my mind.

This question and so many others were circulating through my thoughts. But, the pain in my chest that I was experiencing overtook those questions. This pain felt so familiar to me. Because of this familiarity, I feared that my potassium levels were low and I was on the verge of fainting again. So, I said to the nurse, "Could you please, check my potassium levels? It doesn't matter what's in me or what's going on with me, but I really need you to check my potassium?"

The nurse maintained that is was just the chest tube. But, I begged him to administer the test. This feeling was too strong. Unfortunately, this was a problem that I had in the past.

So, the test was done. The nurse left the room, and moments later came rushing back; his dark skin pale with worry. My potassium levels had indeed dropped dramatically. It was said that I was extremely fortunate to be so in tune with my body. I was able to point out the problem in time. Potassium shots were given to stabilize my levels and everything was back to normal. Well, as normal as things could be for someone with a chest tube sticking out of her chest.

My mind again started to pounder—*Wait a minute; a chest tube? A chest tube due to fluid in my lungs. How did fluid get in my lungs? I'm lying in the bed in the unit known as Shock Trauma because my body has been traumatized. Traumatized by what?*

What happened? My body was traumatized because I became a victim. **I was victimized.**

"I was the victim of a life altering act of vengeance this morning at 6:20 a.m. as I tried to start what was supposed to be a glorious day."

As I laid there staring at the walls, in the bed on the Shock Trauma Unit of the hospital, my thoughts are set adrift trying to figure out what had happened to me. I remember leaving, feeling great, and out of nowhere it happened.

Chapter 2
The Attack

The attack happened on November 6, 2004 early in the morning as I was leaving my mother's home. My son and I were staying with her and my step-father because I was going through a separation from my husband. There had been difficulties in our marriage for a while. Therefore, I felt it was best for my son and I to leave, for our *own* peace of mind. It had been five weeks since we left.

The morning was cold and crisp, yet I was happy. I was happy because the night before my husband and I had met with a mediator to help facilitate the ending of our marriage. The meeting had gone well; as we were able to come to an agreement, to be the best parents for our son.

That November morning, I was cheerful and was mentally ready to work a double shift at the juvenile detention center for girls. I was preparing them for the Dance Battle of the Units. As a dance instructor, I was primed; having choreographed one piece for each unit, so that no one would think I was giving preferable treatment to any one unit.

The music and the dance combinations were arranged and ready to go. I was styling in my new burgundy track suit—usually I wore grey. I felt great. My natural hair was out; I was looking good and was excited to start this new chapter of my life.

However, someone had a different plan. As I closed the door behind me, a man dressed in all black jumps out from behind the bushes pointing a gun at me. I look into his eyes and realize that I was staring into the face of my husband. He says to me, "Get in the fucking car!"

Seconds ticked by as I thought about his abrupt request. Getting in my car would have been the worst decision I could have made. The car was in bad shape. Having been damaged in an accident, the driver side door was jammed shut. In order to drive it, I would have had to go through the passenger door and slide across in order to get into the driver's seat. The vehicle also had power steering issues, so it took time and a great deal of difficulty to back out of the parking space. The crazy thing is, he was aware of all of this!

In those seconds, I had to make a quick decision. That decision was for me to get away by any means necessary. In my hand was a cup of hot chocolate and my key to escape, or so I thought. I fling the cup at him in hopes to scold him, and to by some time. Unfortunately, the lid stays on; the cup just hitting him in the chest then falling to the ground.

I took off running but didn't get very far. My son watching through the window starts screaming, **"Mommy, mommy, mommy!"** By the third 'mommy', I turn around to see what's happening, and a flash of red light pierces my eyes. At that point, my body stiffens going cold as I fall to the ground.

I knew I had just been shot. I knew something was wrong. I also knew that this was not the end; there was no way on this earth I was going out this way. To stay alive, to stay aware, I began to think and pray. *What's my name? How old am I? What's today's date? What's one plus one? Two.*

Seconds later, I see my husband stepping over me stooping down beside me, while putting the barrel of the gun to my head; asking again, "Where's my fucking son."

He continued speaking, but what he was saying was unclear. I could only guess that my lack of hearing him was due the trauma that my body was enduring; the shock to my system. The only thing I could do was stare up at the sky and pray to God. "Please don't let this be the end. Please don't let this be the end. I cannot go out like this." To my horror and complete surprise, he leans down and deposits a kiss on my lips. I was absolutely shocked by this term of endearment. He callously shoots me, and then he kisses me! What the hell!

Suddenly, I get a boost of energy and I am able to get up. I take two steps. My mother comes out of the condo. He then runs up to my mother putting the gun to her stomach, and then to her head. He yells, "You want a piece of me! You want a piece of me!"

For a moment, everything was just still. I so wanted the moment to end. It ends with him pointing the gun at me, delivering four more shots and my body again falls to the ground. He runs off.

Suddenly, sirens can be heard in the distance. Then the police and paramedics came, asking everyone—including myself—questions; all the while, securing the site. My stepfather hovers over me with my son in his arms, asking questions of his own. Unfortunately, my body was not cooperating. My voice apparently lost in the shock my system had just endured.
Soon, numbness began to take hold in my legs, and I had a difficult time feeling them. In a flash, I was strapped to a gurney and placed into the

back of the ambulance. The paramedics fuss over me as we make our way out of the parking lot. We turn the corner, and then nothing. Everything was dark.

Notice Me

Chapter 3

Thoughts

Madness enveloped me as I woke up in the hospital after having being air lifted to Shock Trauma. Family and friends surrounded me as my thoughts returned to the attack. I was wondering why all this had happened. As I communicated with those around me, my first concern was not of my own well-being, but of the girls at the detention center. I was able to think about others since I was not in any pain;

nor did I have an understanding of what actually had happened to me.

Everyone around me couldn't understand that I was more concerned about my job than myself. But those girls depended on me. I love to teach dance. Dancing allowed me to inspire people to express themselves through the magical movement of dance. Dance subconsciously gave them the empowerment of positivity and teamwork. I always took pride in my work. I took pride in the fact that I could still make a difference in those girls' lives.

It was very important to me that the staff and most importantly the girls knew I was thinking about them. The last thing I wanted to do was disappoint them.

Later after surgery, I was sitting on my bed thinking about what had happened to me; "*how did I get here; and why am I sitting here in Shock Trauma?*"

Yeah, I understood that I had been shot; the bullet holes that racked my body was proof of that. I understood that I was in bad shape, the metal attached to my face that held my jaw together was proof of that. The sad reality is that I knew I had just become a victim. I became another victim in the growing world of domestic violence. Why was I made to be a part of that world? To this day, it is still a mystery. It's a question I ask myself every day. But still, *Shock Trauma?*

Still lying there, new questions arise. *How do I get through this? How do I get through this new beginning, this latest journey that has been set before me?*

You see, technically, I had already been on a new journey that day. I had prepared a fresh start for myself and my son. After dealing with the stress and negativity that came with living with my husband, I knew it was time to move on. We needed our own place. We needed our own space to breathe. We needed a safe environment to grow, thrive, and to prepare for the future. *At least*, that was my intention.

I had a good job, working for the state. I was making enough money for my son and I to be able to survive in our own place. I had the freedom to have things of my own. I had *the resilience* to take care of my responsibilities as a mother and as a woman.

So, there I was starting a new chapter in my life. Coping with a separation from a man I knew I could no longer live with. Free to start the divorce proceedings that would hopefully end in an amicable split. All the while being the best parents we could to our son. However, I had no way of knowing my plans would irreverently and perpetually be forever changed. In that hour after the attack, that hour of chaos, that hour of absolute incredulity, our lives had been transformed.

At some point in the early hours of my arrival at the hospital, I had been promised protection; I was promised peace. I had no idea, at the time, why the hospital staff had said this to me. But later, I was informed that my husband, the man who had shot me, was in the same hospital; an unforeseen surprise indeed. What was more bewildering, was the fact that he was here because of an injury. Confusion overwhelmed me. I was the one who was attacked, I was the one who was injured. *Why was he here? How had he been injured?*

Those questions were answered the next day, when I was informed that my husband had passed away. The peace I had been promised the day before, at that point, became my burden. Eyes blurred with peaceful tears; my heart filled heavily with pain. After all, he was my husband, and I did care about him. But I was extremely furious with him, dare to say, hated him even. I was so incredibly disappointed by what he had done to me, to himself, to our son. His death was a result of a bullet to his head; by the very gun he used to shoot me; by his own hand. He had taken his life, leaving our son fatherless, and leaving both of us with the burden of the chaos he created.

As time passed, I was left with even more questions. *Why did we have to go through this? Why did this domino effect have to lay on the shoulder of a young innocent child? Our child!* Our family, our friends, everyone we knew had adversely been affected by this; and still to this day, suffer from it. I could not comprehend why these disastrous decisions had been made. Why the irrational and irresponsible decision that he ultimately made had to rest entirely on us.

So, we all suffered through the pain; we all suffered through the heartache; we all suffered through the anger. We all suffered the same question of *Why? Why did this all happen?*

But for me, there were even more questions; the questions of *where did he get the gun from? Where did he have the gun? How long did he have the gun?*
All these very necessary questions, we asked, I asked; go unanswered. We will never know. I will never know. *Unless?* Unless those answers can be explained by someone he told. Unless the person who gave him the gun in the first place becomes guilt-ridden in his decision to let him have and use it.

My only hope was that my husband's intentions for having the gun were for his own protection; and not because of me, because of something I said or did that he disliked.

Here I was, overflowing with questions and uncertainties while lying in this place known as Shock Trauma.

Notice Me

Chapter 4

Shock Trauma

For those who have never experienced Shock Trauma, or aren't sure what it is, let me explain. Shock Trauma, or a trauma center, is a hospital or unit of a hospital that is equipped and staffed to provide comprehensive emergency medical services to patients suffering traumatic injuries; such as brain injury, amputations, and spinal cord injuries to name a few.

Centers such as these grew into existence out of the realization that traumatic injury is a process unto itself; which requires specialized and experienced multidisciplinary treatment, as well as specialized resources to accommodate patients in need of such care.

Motor vehicle accidents, falls, and assaults with a deadly weapon are the leading causes of trauma injuries. Which leads back to my story.

Because of the cowardly act of one individual who assaulted me with a deadly weapon, I find myself lying in the Shock Trauma Unit with a Spinal Cord Injury causing paralysis from the chest down.

As told by my doctor, paralysis is when one or more muscles of the body lose functionality. Meaning that there is a loss of feeling, or sensory loss, as well as loss of motor functions to the affected area. In my case, I had—*and still have*—paralysis at the T4/T5 level of my spine, which meant that I may have some difficulties breathing, and have difficulty with bowel and bladder control.

As far as breathing difficulties, the only real issue I have is getting enough air to blow up a balloon. But when it comes to bladder control, well, let's just say it's not always a pretty sight. I do manage, however.

The most devastating news was that I no longer had the luxury of using my legs. In the meantime, I would have to make use of a wheelchair since I was unable to stand on my own. Therefore, walking with my son to the park, feeling the wooden surface of the floor as I pointed my toes and danced would be on hold.

All of this went through my mind as the doctor talked and none of it made sense. I mean, I comprehended what being paralyzed meant but it all felt temporary. I still felt movement. I still felt pressure in my legs; therefore, it would all pass.

However, the doctor told me otherwise. He explained that I was still connected to my body, which meant I could still sense the pressure from the compression sleeves. I could still feel the sensation of my legs being moved by others. The connection was lost between the muscles of my legs and my brain, and movement of my legs was no longer possible.

Every day in shock trauma was chaotic. Noise surrounded me, while people were constantly in and out of my room. The ability to think was next to impossible. Even finding the peace and tranquility you need to cope with the trauma that your mind and body were going through was futile.

Sunshine King

Serenity within shock trauma was hard to come by. Family and friends bombard me with love, gifts, and well wishes. Though, they were by my side; they didn't actually seem to be there with me. I could see that their minds are focused on prayers and their own emotional state. Some just stare off into the distance with their facial expression bleak and your left wondering what they are even thinking about. Others are in shock themselves just sitting in disbelief that such a tragic event had taken place for anyone, let alone to someone in their family. I am very grateful for their love.

My peace was put to the test by one family member of mine. They came to me saying that they couldn't suffer through it anymore. They were unable to even deal with being there. They were unable to handle seeing me in the state I was in. I was really at a loss of words, but I had to tell that person to please leave. Thankfully, just like that they stopped visiting me.

Personally, I had trouble coming to grips with this. To me, it seemed really selfish of them to act that way. If you can't stand to see someone surviving, actually making it through such a tragedy, seeing the faith and hope of recovery to return to the life God has preserved for you; then shame on them.

Truthfully, if that person was going to suffer in negativity, I didn't need them around. I was fighting hard to gain peace, to be at peace; and letting that person go without fuss, without tears, was one step closer to that peace.

However, finding tranquility and peace within the chaos while in survival mode was very overwhelming. One had to work hard to find the calm in the storm of what was the shock trauma unit. It's all just one part of the journey.

Chapter 5
Unnecessary Obstacles

Another part of the journey was dealing with all the unnecessary obstacles and complications that followed during my hospital stay for extra care. There were also complications when it came to the health insurance regarding my rehabilitation.

As I am lying in bed in Shock Trauma, fighting to live, I'm hit with questions and concerns regarding my health insurance coverage. I did have health insurance. I had enrolled in the family plan for my insurance through my employer. Plus, I had leave of absence pay—my own, in addition to my co-workers giving up some of theirs to assist me when mine ran out. It was a blessing that I will always be grateful for! Therefore, my stay at the hospital and medical expenses would be taken care of.

The complication came when the resource officer began talking about short term disability verses long term disability. Her explanation was that I did not qualify for long term disability because I had only been working there for 3 years. If I had been working there for 5 years, then I would qualify for long term disability, which in my case was what I needed. She informed me of this in a nonchalant tone, which rubbed me the wrong way. So, I said, "Well, shoot, I should have asked him to hold tight before he pulled that trigger, because if he had held on for two more years, then maybe I could have had some coverage. Are you serious?"

She looked at me dumbfounded. And I looked at her, like "Really?" Then there was that reality moment where you get to thinking, *why would you even say something like that?* It's not like I had a choice as to when my husband was going to lose his mind and shoot me, leaving me in this situation. Needless to say, that was one issue, the policies of the insurance, that had me frustrated in a time when I should be concentrating on my recovery.

Another complication was the fact that my attack happened in the middle of a pay week. That meant the insurance would not be paid in full at that time. Once I was informed of the situation, I felt lost. It was like the doctors were saying, "I want to help save you, but I need my money confirmed first." In my mind, I raged, thinking, '*Dang it, I freaking got shot and you're iffy about saving me! What the heck is this world coming to?*'

The last complication was not having a case worker to deal with all the paper work and all the stress of figuring out the policies of the insurance. Apparently, there was a shortage; whether it was lack of staffing or something else, I don't know. But luckily, I was blessed with a mother who stepped up and took the reins; so that I could breathe and focus on healing my mind and body.

Unfortunately, not everyone has the convenience of having family to step in and free you of these burdens.

Questions did come to mind, while I was laying there in my bed. *What would happen to those who had insurance downfalls such as mine or no insurance at all? What would happen if there was no one there to support them or to help pick up the pieces? How could they manage? How could they even think clearly past their own pain and suffering to even deal with the financial windfall that was placed before them?*

But these questions would have to wait for another time. My focus had to be on me, my healing.

When it came to healing my mind and body, physical and occupational therapy was necessary. Still, rehabilitation came with its own set of obstacles. The first obstacle came in the form of waiting; waiting for a room to become available at the rehabilitation center. Because I was in-patient, it took a little longer for placement. Yet, while I waited in Shock Trauma, I was working hard to get my body prepared for the move. Before they would transfer me to the rehabilitation center, I had to be able to sit up in a chair for at least 30 minutes to an hour without becoming dizzy; that was the goal. The dizziness would come from my blood pressure spiking or dropping drastically during the sitting process; which could cause a person to pass out. Passing out is one sign of Autonomic Dysreflexia (AD). AD is a sudden increace in blood pressure, and if left untreated, it can lead to a stroke, seizures, or even death. Therefore, to assist with my blood pressure levels, they wrapped me from the waist down in ace bandages, as well as compression stockings. All in all, it took about a week for me to accomplish the sitting goal.

Another complication that occurred was how I was going to use the bathroom. This, however, didn't occur to me until my fourth day in Shock Trauma. You see, I had no feeling below my level of injury at that time. So, I couldn't gage whether or not I had to relieve myself. Therefore, every two hours when the nurse would turn me from side to side, they would clean me when necessary. The crazy thing is that half of the time I slept through it from the heavy medication I was on. Needless to say, staying in Shock Trauma for those few weeks was rough at times. Soon, the day came for me to be transferred to the rehabilitation center.

Communication became my next obstacle. After being moved to the rehabilitation center on a transporter designed like an ambulance, I was placed in a room with a lady who spoke Spanish. Now, I was unable to speak due to the braces in my mouth, but trying to understand someone who spoke a different language was challenging.

Soon thereafter, I was moved closer to the nurse's station. This was complicated as well because they had placed me in a room with a lady who had a tracheotomy. At times, she would gurgle and make noises that sounded like she could not breathe, and that scared me. Neither one of us could speak. I was very concerned that if she was having complications, how would I be able to communicate that with the nurses? However, soon, I learned that those noises in her condition were normal. Our communication between us became a collection of hand gestures, like thumbs up, just to make sure we were both alive and well.

Yet, the communication difficulties didn't end there. I assumed that because my roommate and I were unable to communicate by speech, that we were placed closer to the nurse's station to better serve us. So, when we would call for assistance, instead of the nurses coming in to check on us, they would ask us over the intercom system, "How may I assist you?" not remembering that neither one of us could answer. Once they came in, the way I communicated made me feel and sound like I was a ventriloquist. Thank God that only lasted a few days. Once the nurses became acclimated to our needs, things went much more smoothly.

Therapy itself; I can say, I had too many obstacles. I basically had to start from scratch. It was all new to me; trying to sit up, finding my center. My abdominal muscles were very weak, where it felt like I was sitting on a balloon. Understanding what I had to learn and relearn, to adapt to this new life was frustrating. I had to mentally focus and gain self-control just to keep the frustration from boiling over.

My main point of frustration was that I kept getting migraines. Migraines that were caused by the braces that were affixed to my mouth and the poison of the metal that had been absorbed into my system. This is what is known as Metal Toxicity or Metal Poisoning[1]. However, I had to push through as much as I could.

---

[1] **Metal Toxicity** is the toxic effect of certain metals in certain forms and doses on life. Some metals are toxic when they form poisonous

After, a few weeks of complaining, the day came for me to go and get my braces taken off. Once they were off, the pain subsided. However, the complications of having the migraines had led to me missing several of my therapy sessions. Which, in itself, lead to a whole other obstacle; my fight to stay longer at the facility.

Technically, I was scheduled to leave after 4 weeks of therapy, but since I missed some sessions, I had to fight to extend my stay. By fight, I just had to make them aware of the lack of progress in my recovery due to the missed time. After they reviewed my case, and realized that indeed there was lack of progress; I was granted additional time. In the end, I was able to stay an additional three weeks; which was absolutely necessary.

---

soluble compounds. Most often the definition of toxic metals includes at least cadmium, manganese, lead, mercury and the radioactive metals

During those extra weeks, I was taught how to sit up properly, bathe, get dressed, as well as, taught how to manage my bowls and bladder. So, those extra few weeks of therapy were extremely beneficial and helped to make my recovery and transition out of Maryland much more comfortable.

Notice Me

Chapter 6
Flying in Style

I woke up relieved, ready to leave all the stress, chaos, and negative energy behind me. Needing a fresh start and a chance to breathe again. I was extremely excited to begin my new journey.

You know why? Because, this day was the last day! The last day at the rehabilitation center! *Oh, my Goodness!* It was the last day in Maryland and the last day of my old life!

However, as excited as I was for this new life, I have to say that, I was really going to miss some of my favorite staff at the center. Especially, my favorite nurse.

This nurse was someone who stood out among the crowd, someone whose size may have been small, but whose heart was immense.

On the day of my flight, I heard a soft knock on the door to my room. When the door opened, she appeared; my favorite nurse. She came to help send me out on the first leg of my journey. She came with gifts! Gifts that would give me comfort and security of mind throughout the long flight ahead. Along with the gifts, came information.

Now these were not your typical gifts. They were new accessories. The first was a urinary (Foley) catheter[2] that had been added to my

---

[2] The Foley catheter is a tube that helps drain urine from the bladder. It is used by some patients who have had urological or gynecological surgery, or who have a condition that makes urination difficult. If you have a urinary (Foley) catheter, you will use the larger drainage bag at night while you are sleeping

daily wardrobe. Its purpose was to eliminate the constant change of my disposable catheter, which would be impossible to do during the flight. Another addition to my wardrobe were compression stockings[3]. These were provided to help to prevent blood clotting.

After being presented with these gifts, the nurse asked, "Are you ready?" Her question referred to helping me get dressed. Now, at this point I had become independent when it came to getting dressed. However, it took me anywhere from thirty to forty-five minutes to wash and completely dress myself. In this case, because of my scheduled flight, I had time constraints and needed the assistance.

So, I had my fancy black jeans with a pink stripe down the sides and a pink and white top laid

---

[3] TED Compression hose are long, tight fitting stockings that place mild static pressure on the legs to prevent blood from clotting. Following major joint replacement or thoracolumbar spine surgery, the risk of developing blood clots in the legs increases

out. Along with that, my fur coat and pink patent leather boots with a three-inch heel were resting with the outfit. Where I was going, it had snowed, so I had to dress appropriately. The nurse gave me a curious look and asked, "Are you wearing *those* shoes? I responded, "Yes, I have to *fly out in style*!"

Then she said with a smile, "Well, aren't you stylish?"

While in the hospital, my clothing had consisted of sweats and lose fitting clothes. But as I had just explained to the nurse, I'm flying in style; therefore, black jeans and pink high heeled boats here I come. Thus, began the struggle.

Here we were pulling and tugging, left side, right side. It must have been quite a sight. Picture a petite 5-foot, 110 lbs. nurse yanking and pulling, straining to fit the lower half of my body into these form fitting, although not tight, jeans. It was off to a slow start, but once we got going, we were able to get into a rhythm.

Then, suddenly, we were stuck. No more movement, no more progression. At first, I thought I had gain weight and would not be able to roll out in style like I wanted. But then we realized that the zipper wasn't open all the way, and I sighed in relief. Soon, we were done, and I was dressed; ready to go.

As I look back on the event now, I realized the whole experience left me with a new outlook. The old norm of dressing with one foot in after the other, sitting at the end of the bed, was gone. I had lost so much of my independence in a short period of time, which was a large part of who I was as a strong black woman. I had to fight hard to regain my independence back. Now, I had to get used to needing assistance with such normal menial tasks, such as getting dressed. The reality is, this was my new norm.

Maryland had become my cage, a barrier of pain and negativity that I could not escape; and I needed to get away. I needed to separate from where the attack took place. I needed to distance myself from the chaos that surrounded me. I needed to spread my wings and fly.

There were still so many questions; as to why this happened. However, with all those questions, came the bombardment of family and friends (or lack thereof). Don't get me wrong, knowing I had their love and support was great. But it also became overwhelming. During my stay in the hospital, I realized who my true friends were, and it was disappointing to know that people who I thought were my friends, weren't. It really made me stop and think.

As far as my family was concerned, and as much as I know they love me, I felt suffocated. Some were so wrapped up in spiritual and religious materials; to the point where I woke up one day and was surrounded by crosses, bibles, and inspirational prayers. I was thankful but sadly, I felt like I was being attacked at the same time. I felt like I wasn't given the chance to heal on my own way, mentally, spiritually or physically.

Most of the time, I felt like a piece of horrific art. Blank faces stared at me, just watching me. It was uncomfortable, awkward, and weird. Others turned away, not wanting to see the terrifying picture in front of them. One even voiced that they could not stand to see me this way. Eventually, I had to inform that person it was okay to leave. The sadness, the fear, was doing nothing to help me. It was only smothering me.

I had to think about my son and myself. I had to focus on my healing and about how we together as a family would overcome the struggles before us. So, leaving Maryland, to have a change in our environment, was the only way to leave everything behind. It would allow me to become a strong and supportive mother for my son. This change would give us a chance to breathe again; and to soar as a family.

After everything that had happened, I was ready and overly excited for a fresh start, obstacles be damned. I was, however, skeptical about getting from point A—Maryland to point B—New Orleans. Of course, the wings of the plane would get me there. However, I still needed my own mode of transportation, like a personal wheelchair. Unfortunately, my wheelchair had not been provided to me at that time. I was made aware that I had access to a loner wheelchair, and my concerns were put to rest. Having visited New Orleans as a young girl, I knew the climate would be warmer. I felt that's where I needed to heal. I really didn't want to heal in the cold winter of Maryland.

As for personal care; doctors, specialists, rehabilitation; that had all been mapped out for me beforehand. So, there was no concerns as to how to procced with acquiring those assistive faculties. Everything was prepared ahead of time and I was expecting a good transition.

Although, support from family was tenuous. Some were stubborn, set in their ways, and they didn't understand my need to move so far away. I tried my best to explain but didn't want to argue with them. I wanted to keep the peace, to not burn any bridges, and asked that they accept my decision as best they could. Besides, the plan to move originated with my mother and stepfather. It was a plan in which I agreed to. My stepfather, whom had reconnected with an old friend in New Orleans, made arrangements for us. We were welcomed into his friend's home until we were able to find a place of our own. My mother joined me in the move; and along with her, my stepfather, his friend, and surrounding neighbors support, our transition was underway.

Although I was excited and ready to fly away to start my new life; I had to think about how it all, the incident, the move, would affect my son, Isaiah. My son's wellbeing, was a major part of my decision to move down south. Isaiah was still young, 3 years old, when all this took place; and it was my responsibility as his mother to protect him.

Speaking of his youth, I think that helped with the adjustments and changes that was set before him. Isaiah was exposed to the world of disabilities, my life in a wheelchair, in a welcoming way. He was allowed access to the rehabilitation center, where he had firsthand experience with others, like myself, who made use of a wheelchair, as well as others with a multitude of disabilities.

Like all three-year old's, he would be curious and ask questions; and I would give him answers that someone of his age could comprehend. I feel the whole experience allowed him to grow up with the empathy. To gain the understanding to know that the differences in others is not a negative thing, it's just the way of life.

One thing I do remember Isaiah having some difficulty with, was the braces in my mouth. Because of the incident, my mouth and jaw were being held together with metal braces. It was almost wired shut. Although, I could talk, it was hard to do. To show my love I would give my son hugs and kisses on his cheeks. Well, Isaiah wasn't having it. Instead he wanted me to kiss his hand, because of the metal in my mouth. Therefore, he would hold out his little hand, turning his head away as I gave him a kiss on his hand. Afterward, he would look back to see if his hand was still there. All I could do was laugh. I think he was afraid I would bite his hand off. It was understandable. However, after a while, he realized that his little hand was safe from the metal monster in my mouth.

When it came to the move, Isaiah accepted it extremely well. It would be his first time traveling; so, the experience of riding on a train and a bus must have been exciting for him. He went down early with my step-father and was able to see the place where we were to live. In truth, Isaiah was very comfortable with it all. He was even able to open up and talk in depth about his feelings.

By moving down south, it would give us the freedom of a fresh start. I had to adjust to beginning a widow and a single mother with a disability of a very active 3-year-old son. We were all liberated from the chaos and able to spread our wings to soar together in our new home.

Time to fly, doing it in style.

Notice Me

Chapter 7
Moving Down South

I rolled out of the airport in the great state of Louisiana on January 4, 2005, ready to embrace new beginnings in the beautiful historic city of New Orleans.

New Orleans became an easy choice because my stepfather had attended a college there, and he had connections that allowed us to make the move. In Maryland, our current living situation in a condominium on the second floor was not wheelchair accessible, so with the acceptance of a friend of my stepfather, we were able to make the move.

Once there, I didn't think about the fact that my ex-husband, the man who irrevocably changed my life forever, was from New Orleans; actually, he was born there. However, on the second or third day, it hit me, and it was overwhelming. Especially, since everywhere I went and everyone I saw seemed to look like him. Of course, it was my own fears coming to the surface that created these thoughts. Yet, it was very eerie thinking that the faces I saw could have been related to him. Though the majority of his family lived in Maryland, it was very possible that some of his family was still there. I really had to reach down deep, search my spirit, to find peace; to calm myself and realize that I was okay.

Nevertheless, I did not want to focus on that, on him. The purpose of the move, my main goals were to focus on staying alive, being healthy, and finding peace.

One way to accomplish those goals was to find the very best therapy. Since everything was already set up for me while I was back in Maryland, everything went very smoothly. I met with an occupational therapist, a physical therapist, and all the doctors who were to help me in my continuing recovery; and I was happy with the care they provided me.

Back in Maryland, during my rehabilitation, I was given a very thick book on spinal cord injury and resources. It was so thick; I was so intimidated that I didn't even want to open the book. It was presented to me in such a cold manner, that it made me not want to even engage with it. The nurse, who was not my regular nurse, came in, plopped the book down on the table and said, "Here's your book. This is your life." I looked at her, and said, "My life is not in that book. I don't know what you're talking about."

I was really taking aback by her abruptness and how rude her words were. And I sat back and thought to myself, no one can figure out their life from a book. So never opened it. However, when I got settled in New Orleans, I finally opened the book; and there was some good information within. But the whole incident, with her slamming this book down, a book as thick as the biggest dictionary ever, left me feeling overwhelmed. I mean, how dare someone say this is your life, now. This was not my life, now; and I was not going to let some book dictate my life.

While in New Orleans, I was introduced to Christopher Reeves' book. It was a small book, no more than 300 pages. It was very easy going, and I was able to digest it without feeling intimidated. Through reading his book, I could understand more about myself and about the journey ahead of me.

Physical therapy was not the only therapy I needed to recover. Mental health and stability were a priority as well. Signs of PTSD were beginning to show, in both my son and I. Once, while playing at the playground, a fire truck with its sirens blaring went down the street. My son suddenly began screaming, "Help my mommy. Please, help my mommy." I was able to get him to my lap, cradling him in my arms; assuring him that I was alright. But, the whole episode broke my heart.

I realized, as well, that I was also going through PTSD. Once it became dark, I would feel a sense of unease when I was by the windows.

Finding a counselor in New Orleans that was suitable for his age, was problematic. However, I was still in touch with my grief counselor from Maryland, so we were okay. We talked with the counselor weekly by phone, sometimes alone, sometimes with family present. And together, with everyone involved, all the therapists, doctors, and family, I was able to stay on a healthy path to both physical and mental stability.

With all the help and my own perseverance, I was able to get stronger and more independent. So, I felt it was time venture out and work on schooling, for both myself and my son. He was due to start Kindergarten soon, and I needed to find my way back to the working world. My mother and I prepared to enroll part-time in college. The elementary school was only a block away from our home; and it was easy for me to drop Isaiah off, attend classes, and then pick him up afterward. Therefore, it actually worked out for everyone.

During this time, I was continuing my therapy with a Massage Therapist/Reiki Practitioner/Acupuncturist, who helped educate me about holistic therapy. In addition, he helped with pain management and becoming pain free; since I had taken myself off the eight types of medications I had been prescribed. In fact, by the third session, I was pain free, and soon after that, free of the toxic chemicals that affected my system. The therapist was truly an inspiration for me to pursue other avenues outside that of my chosen career path; made me more open to explore holistic therapy practices.

While my doctors and family were my main source of support, I was able to make some new friends during my stay in New Orleans and they soon became part of my support group.

Though I did meet a few people, it was a bit challenging. Most would look at me strangely, and I wasn't sure why until someone explained it to me. The truth is, some people aren't used to seeing someone of such a young age (I was 25 at the time) with a disability. Usually, you see elderly with disabilities, using their canes, walkers, and scooters. So, it was difficult to connect with others, especially someone close to my age.

But I did manage to form a friendship with a gentleman, whom I'll call Big J, and his family; and to this day we still keep in contact. I met him in physical therapy, where he was in treatment for a C2 injury. I really connected with him, and learned a lot from him. His injury was a reminder of my own injuries, and how I could have been in his condition.

Sunshine King

During the incident, a bullet had struck my neck in the C2-C3 region of the spine and missed the spinal cord by a hair line fracture. So, by being around him, I realized what my situation could have been. And we were able to be a great support, both mentally and spiritually, to each other because of our shared situation.

Not that he let anything get him down, though. Because he always had a smile on his face, and worked diligently to get stronger. Which was a great motivation for me to do the same.

Physical Therapy, although it was a source of social activity for persons with disabilities like myself and Big J, it was not the only source. Along with Big J and both of our families, we socialized like any able-bodied person. We attended his family cookout. He informed us about a few festivals too. We also frequented a variety of stores and markets. And even if I was not with friends, I would venture out to other places; like the park with my son, Isaiah. We, as a family, even attended summer math and reading groups.

I also attempted to obtain my driver's license; though that didn't turn out to well because of lack of stability in my back. So being disabled did not stop me from having a social life; and just like Big J, I went out with a smile on my face determined not to let anything get in the way.

These social activities and outings were part of my healing strategy. They were a way for me to become more independent both for my own wellbeing and as a part productive member in the community. Really, it was a way for me to become me again.

I needed to learn how to navigate life in a wheelchair. When going shopping; I needed to determine what aisle to use, ascertain what was and was not accessible. In moving across different areas; I had to figure out how to maneuver over cobblestone, soil, and gravel. My mother and I didn't do much traveling away from home or places I was unfamiliar with because of these navigational hazards, but it all was beneficial to my growth. I didn't want to be stuck in the house, sheltered, and unable to experience the greatness of life.

One greatness of life, the one that meant the most, is my son, Isaiah. Part of my goals, in conjunction with staying alive and being healthy, was finding peace for my son and I; for us to come together as mother and son, to put the past behind us, and to become a strong, happy, and fulfilled family unit. And that is what this move did for us.

After spending so much time in the hospital, I had missed so much with him. He was going through toilet training, he was developing this little personality, and he was growing up way too fast. So, were really needed this time to bond, to reconnect with each other. It was so nice just to have him climb up in to the bed with me, or sit in my lap while I was in the chair. And, we really enjoyed tossing the ball around the house, playing softball.

Also, because he attended therapy classes with me, being disabled became his norm. We were able to communicate with each other about different types of disabilities, and he was able to understand that disability is a part of life, it's not something to laugh at or make fun of. That persons with disabilities are no different than anybody else and should be treated fairly. And he grew up knowing and comprehending these things.

He was so good at adapting to people's needs without questions, and without knowing it he taught me to do the same. Because I knew I couldn't be selfish. My disability was not his fault, so I had to adapt to him; make sure his needs were met. And although, I was tired and sore, when he asked, I would get down on the floor with him, become a part of his world; to play cars or even just to watch cartoons.

We both made the effort to adapt to each other's needs, which helped us to create a firm bond of love and understanding.

Adapting was something my family and I had to learn to do. Because adapting is apart if life. But adapting became a necessity, because we were about to experience out next big obstacle; Hurricane Katrina.

Notice Me

Chapter 8

Preparing for Katrina

Hurricane Katrina was one of the worst storms to hit the United States. In fact, according to news reports across the country, it was one of the 5 deadliest storms to ever hit the country. It started out as a tropical storm over the Bahamas, and then hit Florida. Only to head back out to the Gulf of Mexico to strengthen to a Category 5 hurricane with winds topping at 175 mph., just before making land fall again over Louisiana, Texas, Mississippi, and Alabama.

In Louisiana alone, over 1500 people were killed by the storm and the resulting flood waters. Homes and business were destroyed causing millions of dollars of damage. And thousands of families were displaced, uprooted by the storm, and just trying to survive. My family was one of them.

Before the storm, my family and I were already packing. A cousin of mine was getting married, and we were getting ready to go back to Maryland to attend the wedding. We even had a flight and hotel booked, as we were excited for her big day. While packing for our trip, we heard of a tropical storm brewing in the Atlantic. A few days goes by as the storm grows closer the U.S; when suddenly, we hear that what was once tropical storm Katrina had now been upgraded to hurricane Katrina, and it was headed in our direction.

On the Tuesday, before the storm hit, we were frantic about the impending hurricane. While watching our local broadcast station (we didn't have cable), listening to them talk about the changes they were putting in place to ensure a safe and organized evacuation (if it was needed); we were running around unpacking and repacking for survival. This took "change of plans" to a whole new level. I made sure that I had all the medical supplies I needed. As well as, made sure my son had some things too; such as, clothing and a few toys to keep him happy. All the while, we're worried about how we would get out without having our own personal transportation.

Wednesday comes, and the meteorologists are now certain that Katrina is going to hit New Orleans. Our original flight to Maryland was scheduled to leave on Thursday. But now, the airports have cancelled all flights coming and going out of the area. I understood canceling the inbound flights. Who would want to come to New Orleans during a hurricane? But, why the outbound flights? That was everybody's way out, right?

So, now, here we are unpacking and repacking again. Only packing the necessities. Only packing what we could carry on our backs.

It is now Thursday, and Government Officials are announcing that we are in a State of Emergency. However, evacuations are still voluntary. There seemed to be no urgency in what was going on.

An uncle of mine, who is a truck driver and watching from elsewhere, kept telling us that we needed to get out. He was saying that the forecasters were calling for 30 to 40-foot waves that would submerge the city. That was very important information to know since New Orleans is under sea level. Yet, at the time, that was not what was being said in New Orleans. So, again, no sense of urgency.

Watching the news, I began to understand what the people of New Orleans meant when they said, "Hurricane Party". While watching the news we saw reporters on Bourbon Street interviewing people who were obviously drunk; people who were turning the storm that was coming our way into a reason to party. Again, where's the urgency, the seriousness?

Well, the urgency was with us. My stepfather started calling cab companies, and they informed us that because of the circumstances (State of Emergency) that they would be able to take us wherever we wanted to go; for a fee. We were informed that it would be a flat fee of $180 going from New Orleans to Baton Rouge.

(Normally, because of my disability a cab ride cost next to nothing to get me from one place to another) At the time, my money was held at a local bank with no access out the city of New Orleans; So, I emptied the account to have funds. Since the power would be out due to the storm, it would not make sense to keep funds there. The decision to leave using the cab services was made.

Our destination was clear. We were informed by a friend of my stepfathers, who happened to be a nurse, that a University in Baton Rouge was to be transformed into a special needs shelter. Baton Rouge was only about an hour and half travel from New Orleans, on a good day. Therefore, the university was where we were headed.

It's now Friday. Officials call for mandatory evacuations; a decision I think was too long in the making. News stations are dictating the proper evacuation procedures; what Parrish's (county's) were first, then second, third, and so on. Then once each Parrish were empty; how to follow each stage thereafter.

Our cab arrived early Sunday morning. Myself, my son, my mother, my stepfather; we all pile in for our trip. Now, we knew that in the current state that our trip was going to take longer than an hour and a half. So, we considered our options.

We knew the Superdome was being used as a last resort "safe haven or shelter" for those who were unable to leave. The mayor, during a news report, emphasized that people needed "to leave the city." Mentioning, that the superdome would not be a comfortable place, but it was better than staying home. The mayor also informed people that "the dome would be without power and water for a few days or even weeks" after the storm hit. Later during the same report, the schedule for intake at the dome was announced; indicating that the doors would open at 8am to 2pm for special needs and their caretakers, then from 4pm to 8pm the doors were to open for the remaining populace. This arrangement would have separated our family; so, we decided against it and continued with our original plan.

The University in Baton Rouge was the safest option for us. It was farther away from the storm; and we knew the facility was set up to accommodate those with disabilities, like myself.

We are now in the cab, leaving. And it is a very eerie, *eerie* feeling. You don't see a bird in the sky. You don't see a squirrel on the ground. You don't see any insects or birds flying about. Nothing. It was like a ghost town.

Sunshine King

People were leaving. It was dead quiet. You probably could have heard a pin drop; that's how quiet it was.

Five hours into the trip, it begins to rain. The outskirt of the storm was upon us. And we needed gas. Further up the road, we find a gas station. This gas station had a line of people that wrapped, at least, four times around the building. This was the cash only line; and for those who were buying gas and snacks. For those with credit and bank cards, it went a little faster. There was a good Samaritan helping out, using his credit card for gas, and accepting cash in return; which helped others out. Luckily, I still had some funds left for gas on my credit card.

We're back on the road, and traffic is moving at a sails pace. The rain started to fall a little faster. The scene before us was disturbing. Cars had pulled over; apparently broke down. Mothers and fathers with their children, their babies, the elderly; they're all just sitting there waiting for help to come. And you want to be the one to help, but you can't. You must keep on moving.

The whole thing was just sad. Here we all are, looking out at these people, and you want to reach out to help. But, there's this glass wall there. And there is nothing you can do.

It's now six hours in, and we are only half way there. We figured that out since we were only traveling about 20-30 miles per hour. The storm has now gotten closer. The rain falls faster and harder. And everything and I mean everything is closed. No more gas stations and no more convenient stores in site. Just endless travel at a slow pace.

Twelve hours later; Yes, twelve hours, compared to the normal hour and half, we arrived at the university. After thanking the driver, who became like family during the ride, and wishing him safe travels to family, we walked into the gymnasium of the university. We were greeted by staff as we checked in. They escorted us to our designated area. A sense of peace set in. It was that moment of calm; the calm before the storm known as Hurricane Katrina.

Notice Me

Chapter 9
Surviving Katrina

On Monday, August 29, 2005, at approximately 6:10AM in the morning, daylight central time, Hurricane Katrina made its second land fall as a very powerful Category 3 storm, with sustained winds of more than 125 mph. The following day, the levees failed, sending flood waters into the city of New Orleans. The roof of the Superdome, where more than 10,000 people sought shelter from the storm, was severely damaged. Those, along with hundreds of thousands more were left without food, water, supplies, and power.

That was not the case at the University, where we were. We had power; generators worked to keep us sustained. We were provided three hot meals per day. The facility was well equipped to accommodate us. We were even provided a television to keep us informed of the severity of the event. And as devastating as it was to see, it was important to be kept up-to-date.

The University, it's shelter, was not managed by any government agencies. It was actually organized by the staff and students of the school who volunteered their time and resources. They worked in conjunction with the staff from nearby hospital; which wasn't far away.

When we had arrived the Sunday night before the storm, the gymnasium; which was huge, only had about 100 people there. So, there was plenty of space. There were cots set up for us to sleep on; which was a little uncomfortable for me due to my condition. But, I made due with extra blankets and cushioning.

As I got settled on the cot in our area, a volunteer came over and asked me if they could borrow my wheelchair. I looked at him as if he had bumped his head. My wheelchair was custom made for me and was a part of my wellbeing, so I said no. He then proceeded, seeming as if he was going to take it anyway, saying that he would bring it back. My voice firm, I explained that my wheelchair are my legs, and that no, I could not assist him. My mother repeated the same.

To keep others from coming up with the idea of taking my wheelchair, we decided to take some of the yarn from my mother's crochet set and tie my wrist to my chair. She always carried it with her no matter what. After that, my nerves were all over the place, and I could barely sleep that night.

When I woke the next day, there were more than 400 people occupying the area. Not only had the population grown, but the gym itself had transformed. Everything had been sectioned off. There was a section for people with paralysis; which was where I was. There was a section for people with Diabetes. And another for people with Asthma. The whole place was organized to accommodate anyone with whatever ailment. They were prepared.

The area was designated for people with special needs, so my stepfather and son had to be moved to a different area of the campus with a few others. One of the volunteers there was a pastor whom escorted them to the other part of the campus which was the chapel. But after the storm, I was told that they had been moved 20 minutes away to another area. Luckily, our cell phones, which were Maryland area code phones, were still working and we were able to keep in touch.

Unfortunately, their accommodations were not as hospitable as mine; no cots; no hot food; no power. Therefore, my step-father had to be very careful with the battery life of his cell phone. The storm took out the power in Baton Rouge too. But they were basically safe, and that was the important part.

The 400+ population at the university, after the storm, grew to twice that much, even more. The huge gymnasium was now packed, and many more were scheduled to arrive. People who had been stranded, surviving on rooftops and in boats, were being brought in to fill the place almost beyond capacity.

What was so unbelievable, so heart-wrenching, was the news. Actually, seeing the flood waters;

its height reaching up and over the second story of single-family homes. Hearing about the casualties that kept growing in numbers by the hour. Watching, as water poured through the crack in the roof of the Superdome that was set up as a shelter.

We watched, my mother and I, in horror and shock; praying for all those people who didn't have what we had. People who went for help, expecting to be cared for; who now had nothing, because they weren't prepared for what happened. That could have been us. We had, for a brief moment, contemplated staying in New Orleans; using the Superdome as our safe haven. That would have devastated us, especially with my being in a wheelchair and needing special care.

So, now, here we are, two days after the storm; and people are being brought in. Reality was really setting in. What once was a safe haven for people who were getting away from the storm, was now becoming a safe haven for people who had been through the storm; who were being rescued, pulled off of rooftops and roadsides. People who actually survived the devastation of the storm.

The stories I was hearing from the survivors were heartbreaking. It took a lot of strength to keep the tears that were flowing on the inside from exploding on the outside. I was one of the lucky ones. I still had my family, though we were separated, we knew where each other were; and we knew we were safe. Throughout the day your meeting people, praying with people, and or staying to yourself at times.

Since the gym at the university was becoming overcrowded, the staff began rounding up the stronger individuals, the ones who didn't need

100% care, to move them to Lafayette, Louisiana. I was among that group. However, we strongly dispute this decision. We had no idea of what waited for us in Lafayette. And, there was no way I was going to be separated from my son, my family.

The Pastor that had been assisting us, assisting my stepfather and son, came to us asking if there was anywhere we could go. We had previously made plans to return to Maryland, before Katrina uprooted us. So, with the Pastor help, we were able to make the arrangements to return to Maryland.

Chapter 10
Red Tape

Before even leaving Baton Rouge, before we were able to transition to Lafayette; we were forced to deal with a lot of Red Tape. More unnecessary obstacles needed to be overcome before we could even return to Maryland.

People were fleeing for their lives, trying to protect their families, a lot of them did not have identification; and they were now being classified as "Aliens".

Okay, so let me get this straight. Everyone who was going through Hurricane Katrina; who had gone through Hurricane Katrina. Everyone who had survived Hurricane Katrina; at this moment, at this time, were now "Aliens".

Now, this was crazy. We were all born in the United States of America. Who cares that some us didn't have all of our paperwork, our social security cards. That did not make us "Aliens". Yet, that's how we were being treated; like "Aliens".

Luckily, I had mine and my son's paperwork; my mother had hers. Unfortunately, my stepfather didn't have anything, he was left behind to deal with all the red tape; having to jump through hoop after hoop just to prove who he was. Again, the Pastor was there to assist him, and soon he was on his way.

We were now back in Maryland. We were invited to stay with my grandmother for a few days; which was a blessing. But that almost would have been a hassle, because there were warehousing laws. Basically, housing more than one family in a rental property, when only one family unit is on the lease, is considered warehousing. Red Tape.

Soon we were reunited with my stepfather and placed in a hotel. Government agencies had partnered together to assist Katrina survivors with a place to stay. The Governor of Maryland even sent his assurances that we, Katrina Survivors, could stay in the hotel as long as we needed. However, it was very stressful because we would see people being kicked out of hotels across the states on the news. We, too, would receive warnings, but no confirmation to leave.

Living in the hotel for an elongated time was very difficult. Conditions were less than desirable. It was cramped, there was no sense of privacy, and living in such close courters became very stressful. And with me being disabled and needing special care, it was that much more taxing. However, we had been provided with two rooms; which were next to each other, and I was grateful. My mother and I were in one room while my step-father and son were in the other. The separate rooms within close proximity to each other allowed me to take care of my personal needs with less stress. So, we waited, residing in rooms that were only meant to be used for a short amount of time; all because we were unable to find housing.

The one problem with finding housing, the red tape of it all, came from the lack of organization and separation of housing. In Maryland, we have programs; which are programs set up to help individuals with limited means to find a home. The problem; it seemed like everyone in the state was on one list, there was no separation for urgent or catastrophic cases, such as mine.

Sunshine King

My question to this was, *why?* What happens to a person or persons who were injured in fires that have their homes consumed? Are they just as displaced as we were and just as in need? We had lost our home, myself living with a disability. You would think that people like that, like us, who lost their home due to the disastrous effects of Mother Nature, should be considered for emergency assistance. But no, there's no separation; no consideration.

The whole system was dysfunctional, and I really think that the situation should have been handled better. I didn't understand why they had put us through that, why all this unnecessary red tape had to be thrown at us.
So, due the fact that we couldn't get on any list, we stayed at the hotel from September 2005 to January of 2006.

During the time living in the hotel, I was able to get back into physical therapy; which allowed us to get out of the hotel at least three days out of the week. A needed break from the confines of the rooms. We also would visit my Grandmother sometimes, giving us more freedom. Yet, the confines of the rooms were not the only reason to visit. The hotel was not equipped with the means to fix meals. So, we would either order in or go for dinner at Grandma's. We were provided with some clothing, outerwear, and food, but with no place to store it in the small hotel rooms, we were forced to decline some of it. Which brings me back to the housing obstacle.

The drama of finding a place to live was very frustrating. So, one day, I sat down with a note pad and made some phone calls. While speaking with one agency, I wrote down all the information they provided me; however, it seemed as though they were unable to help with housing. I was referred to another agency that might be able to help, yet they couldn't. That agency, in turn, referred me another agency.

Again, no help!

After I went through about eight to twelve different organizations, a few leading me back to the original agency I contacted; I realized I had just gone around in circles. Literally, I had made a spiral of notes of multiple support groups all leading to one other and none of it got me anywhere. It was amazing to think that within all these agencies; who I assume, as most people would assume, are gathering grants, and monies, and other amenities to help people in need that they weren't actually using what they had to help. I don't know if there was an obstruction within their organizations, or if they just didn't have the means to help. But no one gave a clear direction of where to go. Red tape surrounded me at every turn, and I was getting worried.

For one, I survived domestic violence. Two, I had survived Hurricane Katrina. Now, I had to try and survive being homeless with a disability, with a child; as well as being the main supporter, financially for everyone in the family. My mother and step-father had not been working since we moved to New Orleans. And, that was very, very stressful. I had to keep myself calm, spiritually; because I felt that I could literally lose my mind. I was stuck; stuck within society, and stuck financially. More Red Tape. Eventually, I was able to get us a place in January of 2006. We, as a family, were able establish a routine. And, I was able to live a more productive life as a person with a Spinal Cord Injury.

Chapter 11

SCI

By living with a Spinal Cord Injury[4], I was surviving a very profound learning experience. Learning; when to eat, what I can and can't eat. Learning; how to take care of myself, my body and my limitations. Learning; to get back to basics in life. Throughout this journey, I have learned a lot about myself and living with a SCI.

---

[4] **Spinal cord injury** is damage to the spinal cord that causes loss of sensation and motor control.

What to eat and what not to eat was something I learned over time. The first six to eight months was a period of trial and error. One thing that didn't work for me was the combination of hot tea, applesauce, and oatmeal first thing in the morning; along with medicated stool softener. For those, like myself, who have a spinal cord injury with little to no bladder control and bowl difficulties, it's just not a good mix.

It's also not a good idea to eat such foods before leaving the house. In my case, during my learning phase, I had ingested these foods just before leaving for a doctor's appointment. So, when I arrived, the doctor had a not so wonderful surprise.

Now, as embarrassing as this was, the truth is, it was a learning experience. Sometimes, it's ugly, but it's a learning experience all the same.

During this trial period, I also experimented with juicing, green juicing to be exact. Because I had already had the previous incident at the doctor's, I decided to stay indoors for three days straight, just to be safe. Luckily, I didn't have any complications. In fact, it was quite cleansing, and aided in the healing of my body.

The importance of taking care of your body is beneficial to the healing process. Personally, I have a background in dance; therefore, I believe utilizing my knowledge of movement through music helped in the healing of my body. Nevertheless, we all must make time to take care of our basic needs; like bathing, checking our skin to prevent from pressure sores, keeping our skin moisturized, and maintaining clean and manicured nails. However, for those with spinal cord injuries, these simple tasks seem monstrous.

No matter how extraordinary the task, it still had to be done. Keeping my body healthy internally and externally was an important goal of mine.

In order to obtain this goal, I had to essentially treat my disability as if it were an infant; as if it were my second child. So, as you would careful wipe down an infant to clean them; I bathed myself. As you would lotion an infant to keep from skin breakage, I moisturized myself. And as you would gently clip the fingers and toe nails of an infant; I manicured myself.

Dressing was the same; in regards to dressing an infant. You want to make sure everything fits. You don't want your clothes to fit to snuggly. It can be quite uncomfortable and can cause skin damage. You don't want your clothes to be to baggy. You could look unkept, unruly, and can be dangerous. The last thing you need is to get your clothes caught in something that could cause you more harm. And just like an infant, getting dressed while lying in bed is faster and easier verses getting dressed in a chair.

What type of shoes you wear is important too. Just like a child, you don't want their feet to grow funny or become deformed. So, I make sure that my shoes are right; that my toes are not squished up together in my shoes. For SCI individuals, like myself, it might be a good idea to wear a half size to a size larger in case of swelling. That was something I learned.

Sitting in a chair all day can be tiresome, and stressful on my body. Just like someone who sits behind a desk all day and has the need to stretch; I too have that need. My bottom often falls asleep. My lower back often gets tight.

Going back to the basic learning techniques of dance, I recalled the movements that allowed me to stretch and strengthen my body. So, I incorporated that into my morning routine;

which, to me, is very important. Every morning, I give thanks to God for keeping my family safe throughout the night and for waking me up to see another day. Then, while lying in bed, I stretch my legs out straight, placing my head on my knees and reach for my feet. Afterward, I kiss my legs praying to them and reminding them how much I miss them. Also, while moving and extending them with my hands, I voice how grateful I am to still have them.

Once, at an event, I noticed a majority of people had their legs tucked up underneath them as if they didn't exist. I was told that having their legs out of the way allows for the wheelchair to fit in small places. To me, this is ridiculous. Your legs are still a part of what God gave you, even if you may not be able to use them to get around.
The rest of my routine consists of me stretching the remainder of my body to get rid of the tiredness.

Subsequently, every day, was a learning experience. I had to give myself time to learn, to explore what worked, what didn't work. And once I become comfortable with what I learned, I choose a routine that fit with me and my lifestyle. So, my advice to you, no matter your disability, is to do the same.

Find what is healthy for you, find what works for you; and stick to it.

Remember, it's all a learning experience.

Notice Me

Chapter 12

The Experience

The experiences that I wish to share are a gift to you. In learning, how to rebuild my body, and believing that things are healing; that was an experience. In paying attention to things like deeper sensations or regaining feeling back in the bottom of my feet, between my toes, under my toenails; that was an experience. In returning back to school to become a massage therapist. In coping with the stresses of transportation and provided services; that was an experience.

All these experiences; these personal things I went through, I treasure. So, let me share my treasures with you.

Throughout these past thirteen years, I have grown a lot in understanding my body and how it works. Seeing and feeling that growth has been amazing. I went from not feeling anything in my lower limbs, to experiencing deep pressure feelings. I went from having bad spasms to learning to control them.

Once my injury occurred, I had to figure out how to deal with the feeling of the loss of sensation. I had to learn to understand the odd sensations of tingling going down my legs. And I had to accept that I could not move my legs. However, I remembered having the same occurrences before my injury when my potassium levels were low. So, the experience wasn't entirely new to me.

As a result, to the low potassium, in the past, I had lost feeling in my legs. One day, I noticed my chest was hurting. I didn't understand what it was because I was working out and eating healthy. It wasn't painful, just a heaviness; a pinch that occurred off and on in my chest. It had been occurring for about three days.

That day, my son and I had just come home, and I had to use the restroom. I remember placing him the crib; then, the next thing I recall was my two-year-old son trying to wake me up. As I laid on the floor, he was forcing my eyes open with his little hands saying, "Wake up mommy, mommy wake up." Once I gained clarity, I noticed it was dark outside; having no idea how long I was out or what time it was. I tried to get up and realized that I could not move my legs. It felt as though my legs fell asleep on me. Eventually, I army crawled to the living room with my son following me;

explaining to him how to open the door and get help. Thankfully, my son was calm through it all. By going through that; then, it helped me to appreciate the journey ahead of me. Nor was I completely devastated by my predicament; because of this previous experience.

I believe that this earlier occurrence happened for a reason. It happened to prepare me, to make me stronger mentally and to assist me in remaining strong in order to deal with the effects of my SCI. If I hadn't had the previous incident, I don't know how I would have been able accomplish or achieved the goals I set for myself over the years.

By undergoing physical therapy and understanding my body and being determined to reconnect with my body, I eventually started to regain some sensations. It has all been a great experience, every moment a treasure.

Making the decision to go back to school for massage therapy was a very interesting experience. When applying to the school, I had an interview with one of the staff members about why I chose massage therapy. The interview went well until the interviewer asked me in a sarcastic tone, "How exactly do you plan to do massages?" I then informed her, "Well, the same way that you do, but from the chair."

I attended classes with no problems, but it felt like she was just waiting for me to suffer through obstacles. However, I did very well and became the first person with a spinal cord injury to graduate.

While attending classes, I was able to get my body worked on; and it felt so wonderful getting massages and receiving mild therapy. Being able to feel the connections within was so liberating. My lungs, which felt as if they were trapped, were finally free. After being introduce to the myofascial release technique[5], my rib cage opened up, allowing me to breathe better.

Now, dealing with the local accessible transportation services was and still is a struggle; and quite an experience. There are transportation services across the country that assist people with disabilities in getting to and from doctor appointments, school, work, the mall, the grocery store, and more.

In Maryland, it's a twenty-four-hour service. However, in other states this service is only available from 5 am until 9 pm. After nine getting to places was a challenge. Therefore,

---

[5] Myofascial Release is a safe and very effective hands-on technique that involves applying gentle sustained pressure into the Myofascial connective tissue restrictions to eliminate pain and restore motion. Myofascial release (or MFR) is an alternative medicine therapy that claims to treat skeletal muscle immobility and pain by relaxing contracted muscles, improving blood and lymphatic circulation, and stimulating the stretch reflex in muscles.

getting used to the differences in multiple states was an experience.

The accessible van services, or as I call them "Mobility Blues" is a whole story in and of itself. Sometimes the service works in our favor and sometimes it does not. Sometimes, it picks us up at our scheduled time; and sometimes it will pick us up an hour or more later. Sometimes the dispatcher will record your pick-up time wrong, and then won't adjust it; leaving you stuck at home. Why you ask? According to their policies they can't make same day bookings, and any changes would constitute as same day bookings. (Personally,) I feel this is absurd especially since "THEY" were the ones to mess up the clients' rides.

Then you have the drivers of the accessible van service. Some drivers are ignorant, being mean and rude for no reason. Some are unkept and don't' care, only there for a paycheck. While others are humble, people who really want to be there out of the goodness of their heart.

Long story short, the accessible van service is an experience that I and others with disabilities go through daily. Even though, the system has been around for a while, it still needs improvements. For starters, I would love the chance to help change the design of the vans to make it easier for passengers to maneuver. Also, I would like meet with a panel of company leaders and consumers to gather and share other solutions that may help to improve standards. Although, the program has some issues that I think need to be addressed, I feel that it is essentially a decent and beneficial program.

Climbing a rope for the first time in the gym; which happened because a partnership between the gym and my Wheel Power program (Chapter 14), was another fantastic experience for me. It felt so good to relax the vertebrae in my spine. It was amazing to see the strength in my arms, hanging there, looking down at my chair. I was so determined to climb that rope, and I did it. Being out my chair, by my own physical capabilities, climbing up into the air was the ultimate experience.

Since then, I have lost some strength in my arms due to an accident that occurred during a mobility ride where a heavy-set individual and their scooter fell on me. Luckily, I was not injured beyond that; no broken bones, thankfully. But, now, I am determined to regain my strength so that I can climb that rope again. I also had the pleasure in learning about adaptive sports, and went skiing and scuba diving. I even tried out wheelchair basketball, adaptive la cross, fencing, and wheelchair tennis. I'm open to try out more sports in the near future.

Experiencing moving from state to state with a spinal cord injury, surviving Katrina, going through different therapy sessions, and trying out adaptive sports it's all been a journey. It is all a gain in Life. No experience is a loss. No experience is a waste of time. You may question things and wonder why, but it all makes you stronger. It made me stronger.

Chapter 13
Notice Me

The <u>Notice Me Tour</u> is an entertaining show filled with fashion, music, and dance, all performed by a diverse group of professional and amateur models, artists, and entertainers. The objective of the <u>Notice Me Tour</u> is to, of course, entertain; but also, to show that talent is not wrapped up in a cute perfect bow. Talent comes in all shapes, sizes, colors, and abilities. The idea came to me awhile back when I decided to return to modeling with a disability;

and I realized that the entertainment community wasn't adapting to persons with disabilities, as in showcasing actors and artists with real disabilities in print or film. There always seemed to be an actor who had use of his legs playing as a character in a wheelchair, or an artist untouched by abnormality portraying someone with a disorder such as Autism.

In truth, in the entertainment world, persons with disabilities are looked at as liabilities; although that's not the case. People with disabilities live their lives like everyone else, and those with the talent to be on stage, screen, and print deserve the chance to live the life they dream.

After discovering all this, I realized I had to take a stand to fix this. I made it my mission to make sure persons with disabilities were being noticed within the community; hence the Notice Me Tour.

Being part of a community is important for everyone, but more so for persons with disabilities. As part of a physical therapy program, the practitioners always stressed that we shouldn't let our disabilities hold us back. We should be active members of the community and keep a normalcy. For example, going out to shop, seeing a movie, and having dinner at a restaurant. As I ventured out, doing these things, I noticed that I was the only one in these places during that time period with a disability. So, that was when I started to think that more persons with disabilities needed to get out, needed to be involved; at least those of us who could. Those of us who can get out, need to have a voice and have that voice be heard; to be *noticed.*

Being a part of the community is not always easy. However, we, as in those with spinal cord injuries, don't always qualify for things; such as programs designed for persons with other disabilities. I call it being in the Gray Area; not overly disabled, but not able enough. There are some, especially those like me who are independent, who can venture out into the community and get involved. Sadly, there are those who are left behind because some programs are not suitable for our needs.

So, part of my mission, is to reach out to those people in the gray area, who feel like that are lost and have no outlet. To let them know that they have a voice, and that they have a place in the community. Hopefully we all, as a society, can feel more comfortable with our differences; and ***notice*** and embrace each other for the people we are; not the flaws we see.

What I want people to understand is that the Notice Me Tour is not about me. It is about bringing more awareness to people with spinal cord injuries, informing people of the importance in staying healthy, motivating others, informing others with disabilities about different resources available, to Stop the Violence, and to help put an end to Domestic Violence.

Even though I use own experiences, my strength and perseverance as a model for the show, it is all done to benefit others. I want people to notice my strength, and notice my involvement and contributions in the community. The entire production is intended to motivate others.

As an example, I use my story to assist other individuals who want to fulfil their dreams of entrepreneurship, or anything they have their mind set on. I want people to notice me, see that I went through a catastrophic ordeal, and that I'm not going to let that stop me. I'm not going to let paralysis stand in my way of accomplishing my dreams, because I not going to lose myself.

"Because you don't want to lose yourself."

Prior to the incident that left me disabled, I was very visible in the community when it came to theater and dance. However, it was the incident itself, becoming disabled that gave me a voice. It opened my understanding of human equality, and the challenges involved in making those with disabilities noticeable in that forum. Also, I was able to become an extra voice for survivors of domestic violence as I share my story, perform, and model. By doing these things, I am showing that despite going through a horrific situation, I am not going to let it stop me from fulfilling my goals; and neither should anyone else. So, this platform, the Notice Me Tour was created to help people fulfil their dreams, as I fulfil my own.

Sunshine King

As I create platforms such as the <u>Notice Me Tour</u> and contribute to other events throughout the community, I do feel as though I am invisible. There are people around me who see what I am doing, hear what I am saying, and then turn around use it as their own.

This is very frustrating. Since 2005, I take the time to put on a show that is very fashionable and jazzy, using a diverse group of individuals, including persons with disabilities, and showcase the talent of these individuals. Only to have someone pull what they like and use it as a brand-new unique concept created by them.

Therefore, I feel as though myself and the people I am standing up for are being pushed aside, made to be invisible, and not being heard, or being taken seriously.

As an African American, as a part of that community, I notice that we are extremely invisible. When you're watching a show, or looking through some magazines you don't see any African American persons with a disability anywhere. There really is a lack of diversity in the disability community and society; which, is why I personally fight to be seen and heard in the hopes that I can make a difference.

Bringing awareness to domestic violence and stopping the violence is a strong part of the message brought to light through the Notice Me Tour. The facts and statistics of domestic violence are staggering and sadly have not been updated since 2010. But here is what we do know. Every 15 seconds someone is being abused; whether its physically, verbally, emotionally, or financially. Somewhere out there, someone; man, women, and child alike are being abused[i]. Most people don't understand how serious it is. And still others don't know or don't want to know about it. The topic of domestic violence should be talked about, it should be brought to more people's attention, and there should be continued education on what domestic violence is, and how to stop it from occurring.

For those who were or are victims, like myself, it disheartening and frustrating to find help, or even to know how to find help. For me, I didn't know anything about shelters and facilities for abused woman until the last minute, until I was in court trying to get a protective order. If I'm just finding out about programs to help, how many other people out there just don't know.

The more we educate and talk about domestic violence, the more awareness is out there for everyone to seek help if needed; and the more we can take steps as a society to put an end to domestic violence.

Bringing more awareness to persons with disabilities is another message the Notice Me

<u>Tour</u> is trying to spotlight. Before my injury, the only time I saw a person with a disability was on public television when there was a fundraiser being held; or when I was downtown and happen to run into a veteran. I never really saw anyone with a disability who was energetic or upbeat. Most were those who unfortunately had a severe disability and needed a lot of care.

Therefore, when I became disabled, I was introduced to a whole new world. Sure, I knew that there were persons out there that had different types of disabilities, but it wasn't visible in my life. I realized, in comparing my life before and after injury, that we need to bring more awareness to persons with disabilities. I understand now, how persons with disabilities are so invisible to the normalcy of society.

Things could be so different if we could be noticed as a normalcy of society. For example, the entertainment industry, social media, society as a whole would see us as the parents, the homemakers, the athletes, the entertainers, the public officials, and the people we truly are. If these industries use us, as we are, in their works, their magazines, their articles, and their films (even shown as extras), instead of using abled bodied persons to portray us; then we would be seen as part of the everyday norm. The truth is, we are part of the everyday norm.

The Notice Me Tour was created to do just this—to bring awareness to the normalcy of society and to show others like ourselves that we are confident and strong individuals with great talent and amazing minds. We are just as part of society as anyone else; we just do things a little bit differently.

On a personal note, I like to end this chapter with a story and some food for thought. It refers to how people in society can be inconsiderate and not taking notice to the people around them. As a society, people can be very insensitive to others who are different than they are.

For example, one day I was in the store looking at Birthday cards. I was the only other person in the card isle, and a lady comes up beside me wanting to look a particular card that just so happened to be above my head. Instead of speaking to me and using common courtesies, she reaches over me like I'm invisible to grab the card; her bags knocking into me. I instantly moved away, but I had to say something. I made her aware that she could have said excuse me. Continuing to say that if she wanted to get to that particular card, I would have moved out of her way instead of her reaching over me like I wasn't even there. She looked at me incredulously and stuttered something about just wanting look at a card.

At that point, I got a little loud; talking about how we were the only two people in the isle and that she couldn't have the common decency to open her mouth to say excuse me. She just sort-of walked away, flustered, not saying anything.

But here's the point I'm trying to make. Be aware of your surroundings, be mindful of the people around you. Be considerate of other people and their feelings. Be aware that you are not the only one who exists in this world. *Notice* the people of the world. *Notice* the differences that make people special. *Notice* each other. ***Notice Me.***

Notice Me

Chapter 14

Wheel Power Brings You Willpower

As an individual with a spinal cord injury utilizing a wheelchair, my mindset on life had to change. Meaning, I had to understand that I was still able to get around; that the chair didn't take away my personal self-values. I had to understand that being in a wheelchair didn't institutionalize me or leave me house bound. I realized that the wheels below me actually gave me the power of freedom; freedom to explore the world; freedom to expand my creativity, and the freedom to live my life to the fullest.

With this new sense of freedom, came the Intuition of Willpower—the willpower to stay determined and accomplish my goals, the willpower to dream bigger, and the willpower to continue the fight for independence. I needed and depended on the strength of my willpower to be the best mom to my son; and to be the best person for myself, my family, and society. I relied on my willpower to help me become part of the community again.

Sometimes, it takes a lot just to get out of bed in the morning. It takes a lot to want to even get out of the house. And I really had to enlist the strength of willpower to keep me going. That's why I created Wheel Power.

Wheel Power is a dance fitness program specifically designed for persons with disabilities who are in wheelchairs or have lack of or limited range of movement. It's an exercise program full of fun and energetic routines which include fitness and weight training, aerobics, stretching, and all forms of dance; such as ballet, jazz, hip-hop, African, and many others. It's a place for persons from the disability community to come together, workout while having fun, and gain the benefits of a workout without feeling stressed or left out. I created this program years ago, one, because I love to dance (I was a dancer before my injury). And, two, because I noticed a large portion of the disability community was, unfortunately, overweight or obese. Also, as I went about the community, I began to realize that people weren't involving themselves on a physical level as much as they should or could.

There were some groups that were into completive sports. Even within this group, the individuals weren't exercising properly, or using effective breathing techniques to help them sustain their activities.

As I continued meeting and talking to different organizations, I became troubled by the fact that the medications that are being provided for pain relief were filled with extra steroids that actually made a person more susceptible to gaining weight. Of course, gaining weight and how much weight you gain depends on your metabolism and body type; but the sad truth is that the medications you take can cause weight gain.

Therein lies the dilemma, and it becomes a battle. Because, if you are on these medications in order to live your life pain free or more comfortably, then you need to counter the side effects of gaining weight with exercise. And that's not always easy. There are not many places to go where you feel comfortable enough where the exercises aren't appropriate for persons with disabilities. In addition, if you have a personal care attendant, they must to be willing and able to accommodate whatever your exercise regimen is. Unfortunately, a lot of the attendants are not very active, either.

So, it's a fight within the disability community to even push staying active.

There is, however, active bunches within the community who are in the industry to promote exercising, but they aren't seen very often. And, the type of exercising they do still may not be accommodating for everyone.

In the disability community, I see these pockets. Small areas, where they're thriving with energy. Others, where they're under a cloud of dismay; just going by floating along through life.

With Wheel Power, the program is designed to give you the desire to want more, to want to do more. And to me, wanting more starts with exercising; breathing, and stretching. Taking fifteen minutes out of your day to do something that could lead to a stronger, healthier, and more fulfilled life.

One thing I learned, "If you don't want to call it exercise, you can call it *fun sweaty activities.*"

Wheel Power was also designed to provide us with a sense of community—we are all in one place, together, motivating each other, free from judgement, and accomplishing our goals to get moving. We must not be stagnant.

When your moving, surrounded by others with the same objectives, your self-esteem builds. You gain the confidence in yourself to be willing to go out and be a part of your community. You have the enthusiasm to take charge of your life, set personal goals for yourself, and strive to achieve them. Even going to a doctor's appointment, you'll feel better about yourself and feel better about going.

Wheel Power is a place for persons with disabilities in wheelchairs to have a place of comfort and acceptance; a place to fit in while getting the appropriate exercises you need to thrive. There are plenty of gyms and places with exercise programs, but when you get there, you don't see anybody with disabilities or in a wheelchair. As a person with a disability, in a wheelchair, I don't fit in; as many others in my position may feel as well. There's a lot of aerobic exercises taking place, that is mostly leg work.

"Well, legs not working, dear."

This is how Wheel Power came to be. I had to make exercises and workouts that were adaptable for myself. And if I had to do it myself, then I needed to do it for our community, as well. I needed to do if for others in wheelchairs, others with limitations, so they can participate in an exercise program that accommodates their needs and motivates them to get moving; all while remaining upbeat and fun.

Doctors and physical therapists encourage getting healthy, eating right, and exercising; all to decrease the use of medications and hopefully end the use all together. Of course, you should always check with your doctor before starting any exercising routine to make sure it is safe for you and your body. However, exercise is always the way to go. Once you start, you will feel good about yourself and the doctor will be happy that you followed their advice. All in all, that is the mission of Wheel Power, to bring people from the disability community who have limitations together and have a place for us; to workout, to feel good about ourselves, and to get healthy.

Sunshine King

By creating and running Wheel Power classes, my life has changed greatly. I have an extra power within, an extra fire to keep going. This extra power is needed. Needed for myself; and especially for my son. If I am on constant bedrest, not taking care of myself, my physical and mental health, or my spiritual health; I cannot be there for him as he continues growing into a self-sufficient young man. He should not be responsible for me. I am his mother, and it is my responsibility to take care of him. That is why Wheel Power helps me to stay strong and accomplish my goals as an independent disabled single mother.

In reaching these goals, obtaining multiple certifications, exploring different genres of workout routines; I feel really great. With me being the only one with a physical disability stepping out to do this, it feels wonderful to represent the disability community. Trying to be the voice, saying, "We can do this. We can keep it moving. We can do these classes. We have the stamina." Also, it feels good being a facilitator; making changes and modifying what may be too difficult for myself and others.

Not only has my life been changed by Wheel Power, but according to the testimonies of my participates, it has helped change their lives as well. They are able to get out more, and are able to take part in more community activities. They are also able to move their bodies like they never had before. One testimonial mentioned the fact that they no longer felt like a wallflower anymore when they attended parties and family reunions. They felt more confident about getting in the middle of the dance floor and moving to the music. They had a good time without feeling ashamed about dancing and enjoying themselves.

Sunshine King

Another testimonial said that they hadn't moved this way since even before their injury, that they haven't been moved by the entire experience in a very long time; and it felt good. Their body may ache more, but it's was a good ache. That good ache after a good workout where you're asking yourself, "Oh my god, what is this? Is this sweat? I'm sweating. Oh, this is good." And the best part was that they actually had fun with it.

It's a great feeling to know that although we are disabled, we are still able to be active; that we still have and can have movement. Even if the only thing shaking is your left shoulder, you are still mentally and physically present; still connected in the spirit of the class, of the movement, of Wheel Power.

These, with still others, are some delightful testimonies that were given by people whose life have been changed by Wheel Power.

Wheel Power has great potential to go far. In the near future, I see the program appearing in multimedia; reaching people around the world, in their homes.

I personally can't be everywhere, physically; but I can be everywhere in their household in media. The purpose of this is to show individuals of the disability community in all corners of the world that they can do this. That movement, dance, and fun is possible even with a disability. And, hopefully help them get and stay healthy.

It's bad enough that we have elements around us that we can't control. However, we can control our health; we can control how much movement we add to our lives. So, with the program going global, I hopefully can make a difference in people lives; and start a movement that spreads worldwide—Wheel Power.

Sunshine King

Wheel Power is a program developed under a grassroot organization called Sunshine Project H.E.L.P.; which I established shortly after my incident in 2005, to in effect help with my recovery. The acronym actually stands for Healing, Educating, Loving, and People. That's what Wheel Power was designed for; to help, to heal, to educate, and to love people. The program encourages everyone to get moving, to get healthy; and anyone, whether able-bodied or disabled, is welcomed to take part in the activities. However, the program is specifically designed for persons with disabilities who are in that grey area, who are not able enough, yet not too disabled to qualify for certain programs.

This program is for people like myself who are active or want to be active, who are at least 80 percent independent and looking for a place to stay active, workout, and have fun. And in developing such a program, it helped me to understand as a survivor of domestic violence with a spinal cord injury that there is still hope. It helped; so that instead of lying in bed crying, I recognized that there is still hope to overcome. I recognized that this tragedy hadn't stop me in my own personal growth. Developing this program helped give me the willpower to want more from life, to do more. It helped me to stay focus on my goals, to be the best parent for my son, and to make sure I attack any obstacle with a positive mindset.

In truth, Wheel Power—the power of my wheels—gave me the Willpower—the determination—to get out; to fight the fight of life. With this program, I can show others, both disabled and able-bodied alike, that I found my peace; that I found my inner happiness, and that I can still adapt to life. If I can do it, they can as well. Wheel Power brings you Willpower.

Sunshine King

Notice Me

Chapter 15

The Child That Reached Out

A video that has been viewed by many surfed the web. As viewer after viewer watched it, the video was passed on. And passed on. And passed on, many times over. Until it reached my front door, or should I say my son's social media account.

In the video, a teenage girl sent out a plea asking for assistance in finding her brother who had been missing for 13 years. She was the child that reached out.

One day, as I was getting myself together for the day, fixing breakfast for my son before he was to head out to school. Isaiah comes into the kitchen and askes, "Hey, mom. How come you didn't tell me that I had a sister." And I responded, "Say what now?"

Now, I knew that he had a half-sister from his father side, but I never brought it up. It was not as if I was trying to hide the truth from him. It's just that when the incident occurred, they were both very young. And with everything that had happened, the attack, my recovery, and our move; I had to put that part of our life into God's hands. It was important for me to concentrate on my healing, on our healing.

So, when he came to me that day, obviously upset, I confirmed that he indeed had a sister. Concerned, I then asked him, "What was going on?"

He informed me that he had received a video in a message where his sister was reaching out for help in finding him. He, of course, had watched the video, and then had contacted her the night before.

He hadn't come to me then because the feelings were fresh, and he was very upset and confused. But when he did come to me the following morning, he accused me of lying to him.

At that, I had to correct him, because I did not lie to him. I explained to him that because of their ages, he being three and her being seven, it would have been confusing and difficult to bring it up.

For one, we had moved out of the state. Secondly, I had no idea where she and her mother were. And thirdly, I had no intention of contacting his father side of the family, because to me they were all deceased along with him.

After explaining that his father's relatives were in fact alive, but that I had to cut all ties with them for my own health and well-being, he understood.

However, he still questioned why I hadn't said anything about at all. I went on to explain that it would have been stressful for both of us, especially him, if he knew about his sister yet could not see, talk to, or communicate with her in any way. Though I knew her mother, I had no relationship with her, and had no way of contacting her.

He said, "Oh, Okay. But when were you going to tell me."

And I said, "In God's time. And apparently this is God's time. So, now we're having this conversation."

We then watched the video together. He asked how I felt, if I was upset. And I assured him that

I wasn't. I was, however, surprised that everything was coming full circle. And though I didn't tell him this, I was surprised at how his sister worded the video. The impression I got from the video was that Isaiah had been kidnapped and missing for 13 years, and she needed to find him. But after thinking about it for a while, I figured she was nervous and probably couldn't think of another way to voice it.

Deep down, I wish she had found another way to contact us. And in truth, she actually had. A few weeks before we were made aware of the video, I had received a strange phone call where the person kept asking me how I was doing, never saying who was on the other line. It was very creepy, so I just hung up the phone. But after talking to her, she explained that it was her reaching out, but she was so nervous she didn't know what to say. So, I guess the video was the only way she felt comfortable enough to communicate. And though it was a little long, I felt as though she had done a very good and thorough job.

After the initial surprise of it all, I must say I felt at peace. Because I had put it in God's hands, I had let it go; given it fully to Him. Although, I never forgotten about her. In my mind, I kept her at four years old. Of course, I knew she was growing up. However, in order for me to stay on my mission, focus on my healing and Isaiah's growth, I had no choice but to let it go to God. But now that it was all out in the open, I can definitely say I was at peace.

I was also pleased. It had come at a good time. We had moved around so much since the incident, and now we were stable, and in a good place, so God had held on to it until we were ready to accept this new endeavor in our lives.

Sunshine King

Once Isaiah and I talked and we both came to
an understanding of why things happened the
way they did, I got in touch with Isaiah's sister.
I was happy to talk to her; she had grown up so
nicely. And I explained to her that I was not
mad or upset with her in any way for reaching
out. What she did was needed, for both of them,
to gain closure, to begin to heal. And now since
they made contact, and our families both lived
in Maryland (only 30 minutes away), they could
continue the healing and build a bond.

We were both nervous on that first call, but as
we continued to communicate, and she
understood my point of view, our nerves
subsided.

Before hanging up, I agreed that we would all
meet. However, since Isaiah was having some
issues in school and we needed to combat that
problem, we would have post pone the meeting

for a little while. So, we made plans to meet a month later.

Our plans for that month was to meet at a private location. It would be a meeting with her, her mother, myself, and Isaiah. We were unsure of what our emotions would be and how those emotions would play out in our expressions and behaviors; and we did not want any of it to be publicized.

Unfortunately, the private place was no longer available for us to use, so we ended up going to a restaurant. Happily, everything worked out well. Since the two had been talking through social media and over the phone, emotions were not as overwhelming as first thought.

Her mother and I had spoken briefly before the meeting as well but speaking to someone over the telephone is not the same as meeting with them in person. Yet, the meeting was very peaceful. We all sat together and ate dinner, and talked about the decisions that were made in the past. As a group, we came to an understanding and agreed that we are all on a peaceful mission to unite the siblings so they can grow and bond as brother and sister.

One thing that came up in the conversation during our first meeting was a question that had always been on Isaiah's sister's mind. She asked why I was so standoffish toward her in the past when we would come together as a family to celebrate birthdays and special occasions. Firstly, I apologized to her if I made her feel that way; it was not my intention. Then I explained to her that as a woman, a woman with class, that is was not my place to crowd around or monopolize her father when he was there to spend time with her. This was their time to share, and I respected that. I was there as an extended member of the family to give my blessings and gifts, not to make a spectacle of myself. After clarifying, she understood; and she was able to respect me for the woman I was then and still am today.

Subsequently, when the dinner was over, we all accepted that this relationship was new, and it was going to take some time to make up for lost years due to the catastrophic event. We were all at peace with the past, and ready to make plans and grow the family beyond tragedy.

Although the meeting went well, and a blossoming relationship was established between the two siblings, as well as between myself and my step-daughter; there were some negative effects because of the video. As time went by, I started to receive messages on my online business account. Apparently, fans of the video had done their own research and found my profile. I received several postings stating that I should let the children see one another because neither one of them had anything to do with the incident. Well, by this time, they had already met and were communicating regularly. As a matter of fact, the two had joined up and created a reunion video, explaining everything that had happened. So, these "fans" had not done any other research except to find me to complain; because if they had, they would have known that there was a follow-up story.

In another post, someone called me a Bitch; which was totally uncalled for. Cursing me and calling me out was no way to solve the issue. But then again, we are talking about people who apparently have too much time on their hands and just want something to complain or comment about. I, being an intelligent level-headed woman, did not cater to them. You see, some people are filled with misery and anger, and that's their way of attacking someone. No one deserves to be bullied or attacked on social media, so I left it up to Isaiah's sister to speak to those people to calm the waters.

These postings were on my business profile, however, and it was concerning, because when it comes to people trying to halt my business or stop my growth, I have a problem with that! Fortunately, no adverse effects harmed my business, and Isaiah and his sister continued to make videos and posts to update the fans. Unfortunately, I continued to get harsh comments for a while. The people not taking the time to research and find out the whole story before speaking about something they had no understanding about.

As far as my personal relationship with the child that reached out, my step-daughter, we have a good rapport. We talk periodically, discussing her job choices and schooling, and I give her advice when she needs it. It is still a learning process for me, though, because she considers me her stepmom. And I have to understand my place as her stepmom, since I haven't been there in that role. But the great thing is that we have a lot in common, like hair, make-up, and fashion; all the girly stuff. And it's good to have that there between us to help bridge the gaps, if there be any.

What the future hold for us is unknown, but I look forward to continuing our relationship to find out.

Notice Me

Chapter 16

Making History

Since the incident and my resulting injury which occurred in 2004, I have made my own history. Initially, I am the first wheelchair graduate from the massage therapy program in the city of Baltimore; in the year 2007. When I originally began the program, the instructor looked at me and asked how I was going participate, as in using my hands and giving them a proper massage. And I informed her, "The same way that everybody doesn't, just sitting down." And she said, "Oh?"

So, when we got to a point where there were potential obstacles, I had to figure out a way to adapt; and I did. I didn't let anyone know when I was having difficulties. I worked it out. I was very determined to learn, because I always wanted to be involved in some way in Physical Therapy.

Back in High School, I decided to become a Physical Therapist specializing in dance therapy or sports medicine. So, therapy had always held a special place in my heart.

Before my injury, I participated in the orientation for massage therapy, but unfortunately, I did not qualify for the program at the time. However, after my injury, when I returned to massage therapy, I had a disability and my marital status changed. I had become a single parent; and now, I qualified for grants and loans that weren't available to me previously.

In addition to making history by being the first wheelchair graduate from the massage therapy program, I also became the first wheelchair model in local Fashion Week—2009. As well as, becoming the first wheelchair model presented at an out of state Fashion Week—2016. Furthermore, there were several other shows that I participated in where I was the only wheelchair model. In 2017, I was the first African American Adult model to be featured in the first adaptive clothing line campaign.

These were my personal history making moments, but in my professional life as an entrepreneurial, I have also made history.

In the state of Maryland, and possibly in the entire east coast, I am the first one to have created a wheel chair entertainment group called

Sunshine Models on Wheels. We are a very unique group, and as far as I know, one of a kind. There is no other wheelchair entertainment group in Maryland, and we have been showing off our talents since 2006. It's a great feeling of accomplishment knowing that what we have is special and one of kind, even if we haven't yet been acknowledged on a larger scale the way we want to.

Programs, like the ones I have created and are associated with, I feel, are essential for the disability community; essential for my own continual growth and healing. I need to keep it going, even if it's just me. I still feel the need to educate. I still feel the need to spread my mission of H.E.L.P—Healing. Educating. Loving. People. Wheel Power, which instills strength and confidence, is an important part of my growth and healing; and I will continue to promote its benefits. Sunshine Models on

Wheels, which allows individuals such as myself to showcase their natural beauty and talents, is an important part of my strength in surviving domestic violence; and I will always use my talents as a performer to bring light to the magnitude it has in our society.

By taking part in trade shows, expo's, and demonstrations throughout Maryland, I intend to educate, entertain, and emphasize my message, to H.E.L.P; and to instill the power of hope.

As these programs expand, which is my expectation, I anticipate a certain outcome; Growth. Through Sunshine Project H.E.L.P and its programs, I wish to see everyone, especially those in the disability community, grow.

By educating, people can understand that they can do more, and hopeful have the desire to do more. Through education, I want to see society has a whole grow and fight to expand and create better resources; and make them more readily accessible to those who need it. It's such a shame that we must struggle and fight to get what we need when we know what we are capable of having, capable of learning, and capable of doing in life.

By entertaining, people can have a voice; step out of their shyness and stand up in front of a group and speak. When performing, I hand the microphone to our members, make them speak; and though it's may be only a small group, we are speaking out. We all, as a society, must have a voice. And when we come together, we come together for everyone. It's about all of us. We can help each other, and learn new and wonderful things by coming together and standing up for each other.

Through entertaining, Sunshine Project H.E.L.P has reached thousands of people from different walks of life; showed that we are active and present and living life. And as we continue to travel across the country, we can reach thousands more, hopefully millions; in the hopes that our message of peace, along with healing, educating and loving people will spread and induce understanding and growth in everyone across the world.

The advice I want to leave you with is this. No matter if you were born with a disability, or suffered an injury that caused a disability; ***do not stop fighting to live and enjoy life***. You just have to do it. You have to enjoy life. You have to keep moving. You must get involved in things. You can't just sit around and cry in the corner. ***Get up, Live life!***

Notice Me

You don't want to be bound to a nursing home if you don't have to. Seek out your independence.

Reach out to us; to Sunshine Project H.E.L.P. We will come to you. We have mentoring programs. We have *so many* programs to offer. And we will do our very best in trying to help you get involved, to get out and about. When you join us; you will never get bored. No one has ever said that they were bored. I will most definitely keep you busy, if you want to stay busy.

Once you know me, and the organization, you will never tire of boredom. Just come to me. I will advise you on what can be done. If there something you want to do, I can help you to find a way to do it; so, you can find that happiness, the enjoyment of life again.

Sunshine King

I'll tell you this. The only thing that frightened me was ice. But once you know how to manage it, you can slide on by. The thing is this, ice is slippery and you may not be able to control where it leads you, but at the same time you can manage it. You can manage to be strong and move across it. Or you can wait and let it melt, and then manage to go through it. The point is, in either choice, don't let things get in your way. Don't let ice or steps or any other obstacle get in your way. Obstacles, such as these, can be overwhelming and can make you want to stop doing things; or living life. But you cannot let that happen.

If life is about those elements getting in your way, you have to find a detour. If you can't take the front door, take the back door. If you can't the back door, take the side door.

If you have a support system, you can manage anything. So, find that support system. Better

167

yet, let us at Sunshine Project H.E.L.P be your support system; be your detour, to help guide you over that slippery surface, to help get you over that bump, to help you break down those obstacles that stand in your way.

<u>Don't ever allow your disability to discourage you from doing anything!</u>
<u>Make you own history!</u>   **<u>Stand out!</u>**
<u>Don't follow the Crowd!</u>   **<u>Be Unique!</u>**
<u>Stay awesome!</u>   **<u>Stay Amazing!</u>**
<u>and</u>
<u>Make History!</u>

Sunshine King

Sunshine King is a dedicated activist for disability rights and health and wellness. She has turned her tragedy into a passion that enhances the mind and spirit of people in need of help. Her desire to nurture what ails has led her to become certified as a Reflexology, Massage Therapist, Third Degree Reiki Practitioner, Iridologist, and Life Coach.

Sunshine's refusal to remain a victim after paralysis, has propelled her to remain active in the art's and theatrical industry. She teaches other disabled adults and children how to remain active through adaptive dance and aerobics. She also works as wellness practitioner and entertainment coach teaching modeling, acting, and choreography for various agencies. In 2016, she was invited to "walk" the runway at New York Fashion week. In 2017, Sunshine was the first African American Adult model to be featured in the Tommy Hilfiger adaptive clothing line campaign.

Sunshine is the survivor of a brutal domestic violence attack perpetrated by her then soon to be ex-husband that left her with a permanent incomplete T4-T5 spinal cord injury from being shot four times. This tragic incident ignited a spark that exploded into Sunshine Project H.E.L.P {Healing. Educating. Loving. People} and Sunshine Models on Wheels, founded in 2005. Her organizations' mission pledge is to empower women through the recovery stages of exiting a domestic violence situation, boost their confidence and self-esteem, and educate the public about the often-hidden issues of domestic violence.

Sunshine's diligent work within her community and other states have not gone unnoticed. Sunshine has been honored as a double survivor by local organizations, and has been featured in the Baltimore Sun News Paper, Baltimore Afro News Paper, Carol County Times, Comcast Newsmakers, Inside Edition, MSN News, AOL News, and Story Trender; as well as has had numerous radio interviews in multiple states. Sunshine also has been honored as one of the

Sunshine King

Best-Seller Co-Authors in Kim Coles books entitled *Open Your Gifts-Volume 2*.

Special Thanks—

I must say thank you to my amazing friends and supporters. To Melissa Kendall, for being my amazing ghost writer and secretary. To my right-hand supporters, Vandelia Saunders & Judith Hughes. To my amazing travel assistant, Danielle Edwards. To the lovely book coach, Feleshia Thomas. To the amazing book designer, Tiffany Jeffers. To the lovely Londyn Nikole. And, to the editor, lovely Tracy V. Allen.

Sunshine King

---

[i] According to the CDC and the National Coalition Against Domestic Violence—

> On average, nearly 20 people per minute are physically abused by an intimate partner in the United States. During one year, this equates to more than 10 million women and men.
> 1 in 3 women and 1 in 4 men have been victims of [some form of] physical violence by an intimate partner within their lifetime.
> 1 in 4 women and 1 in 7 men have been victims of severe physical violence by an intimate partner in their lifetime.
> 1 in 7 women and 1 in 18 men have been stalked by an intimate partner during their lifetime to the point in which they felt very fearful or believed that they or someone close to them would be harmed or killed.

To see more visit
www.CDC.gov/violencepervention/pdf/nisvs_report2010-a.pdf

Also visit www.ncadv.org/learn-_more/statistics

www.ingramcontent.com/pod-product-compliance
Lightning Source LLC
Chambersburg PA
CBHW070918270326
41927CB00011B/2621